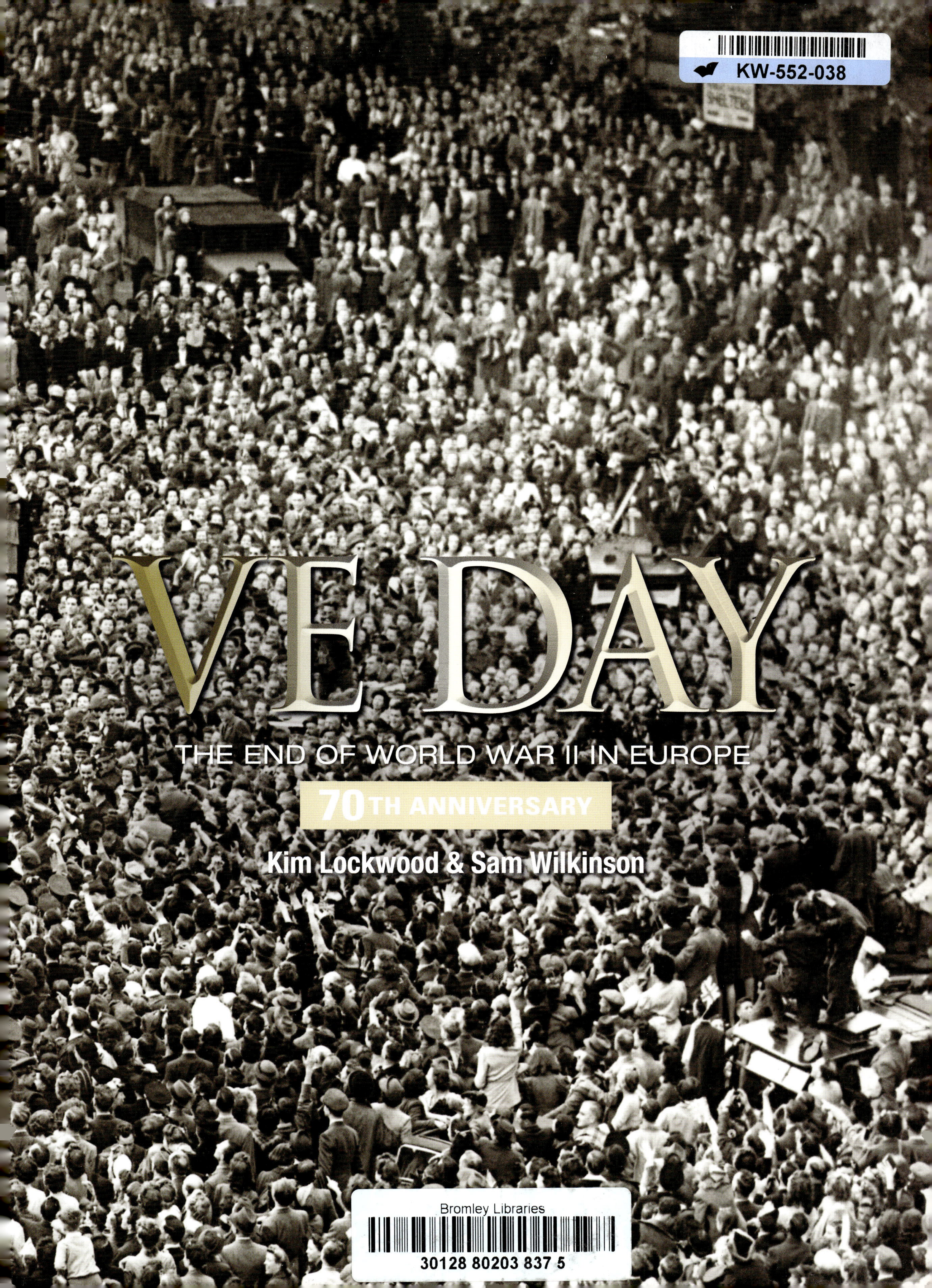

VE DAY

THE END OF WORLD WAR II IN EUROPE

70TH ANNIVERSARY

Kim Lockwood & Sam Wilkinson

Published by:
Wilkinson Publishing Pty Ltd
ACN 006 042 173
Level 4, 2 Collins St Melbourne, Victoria, Australia 3000
Ph: +61 3 9654 5446
www.wilkinsonpublishing.com

International distribution by Pineapple Media Limited
(www.pineapple-media.com) ISSN 2200 – 7926

National Library of Australia Cataloguing-in-Publication entry
Author: Lockwood, Kim, 1944 - author.
Title: VE day : the end of World War II in Europe / Kim Lockwood and Sam Wilkinson.
ISBN: 9781922178855 (paperback)
Subjects: V-E Day, 1945.V-E Day, 1945--Pictorial works. World War, 1939-1945--Armistices. World War, 1939-1945--Europe--Peace.
Other Creators/Contributors: Wilkinson, Sam, author.
Dewey Number: 940.5421

Photos and illustrations by agreement with international agencies, photographers and illustrators including Getty Images.

Design: Michael Bannenberg
Printed in China.

THE AUTHOR

Kim Lockwood is an acclaimed author with a keen interest in Australian history. Growing up in Darwin after the war – his father, journalist and author Douglas Lockwood was there for the bombing on 19 February 1942 – he later worked as a journalist in Perth, back in Darwin (where he lived through cyclone Tracy) and Melbourne, undertaking senior editorial roles for the Herald and Weekly Times and News Ltd. He is the author of or contributor to 16 books, including *Charles 'Bud' Tingwell's War Stories.*

Sam Wilkinson is a writer and editor. His previous title is *Pope Francis: Two Years of Change.* He also works part-time as a journalist on Melbourne radio, and spent several years working in radio in regional Victoria.

When J.D. Salinger scrambled from his landing craft into waist-deep water at Utah Beach on D-Day he was careful to keep a sheaf of papers dry. It was the first six chapters of *The Catcher in the Rye.*

He survived that day. On the second his 4th Division, moving inland behind the beach, lost 20 to 30 men in each field. An area of 100 metres by 100 metres could cost a whole platoon. It was ugly.

Salinger was part of the counter-intelligence corps, whose job it was to interview prisoners of war and civilians, during which he used his proficiency in French and German to find out where machinegun nests were, where a village's alleyways were, where the avenues of fire were. The CIC provided this information to the command posts to help keep men alive.

He was present during the liberation of Paris on 25 August 1944. He met Ernest Hemingway – a war correspondent – and showed him the early stages of *The Catcher in the Rye.* Hemingway liked it.

He was present during the Battle of the Bulge and other big confrontations, serving in five campaigns and earning the rank of staff sergeant.

In April 1945 he entered a liberated concentration camp, probably one of Dachau's sub-camps. He was hospitalised for a few weeks for combat stress reaction after Germany was defeated, and later told his daughter: "You never really get the smell of burning flesh out of your nose entirely, no matter how long you live."

During breaks he worked on his novel and wrote short stories, four of which were published in *Story* magazine and the *Saturday Evening Post.*

The Catcher in the Rye was published in 1951. It has sold 65 million copies. Salinger died in 2010 aged 91.

The beginning
of the end

The beginning of the end of World War II – 5 June 1944 – saw heavy Allied bombing of France's Normandy coast. It was the largest attack by the RAF's Bomber Command in terms of tonnage – 5250 tonnes – up to that point. The bombing left the German defences on Omaha, Gold and Juno beaches almost intact, but did not damage Allied landing craft in the Channel.

As the Americans began bombing Omaha and Utah, the Anglo-Canadian naval forces began bombarding German shore batteries and bunkers. On 6 June the British cruisers *Belfast* and *Diadem* started shelling the Atlantic Wall. The German battery at Longues was the only one to return fire, but was quickly destroyed by the light cruiser *Ajax*.

At 6.10am the 11 destroyers of Force J moved in to begin bombardment, hoping to damage light gun emplacements and stop the Germans moving across the beach. They were supplemented by raids by medium bombers and fighter-bombers of the RAF and USAAF, which dropped an additional 2780 tonnes of ordnance on the landing zones.

As the bombing continued to hit Juno, the destroyers and landing craft began close-range saturation fire. As well as the destroyers — two Canadian, eight British, one French — converted landing craft with 120mm guns provided bombardment. Smaller, light-gunned landing craft got closer to the beach and used their 6-pounders against German defensive positions. Eight landing craft fitted with more than 1000 high-explosive rockets, and 24 LCTs, each carrying four M7 Priest self-propelled guns, also provided firepower.

The bombardment was due to stop immediately before the assault companies landed on Juno, but heavy seas delayed it by 10 minutes. This was at a slightly higher tide, closer to the beach obstacles and mines. The LCTs carrying the field artillery had to adjust course to avoid landing too early. The LCTs carrying DD tanks – "swimming tanks" – had to stop because the seas were too rough to launch them, so they deployed several hundred metres out.

The beaches

More than 150,000 men landed on the four beaches – Utah, Juno, Gold and Sword. Of the 10,000 casualties, more than 4000 died. They were shot. They were blown up. They drowned. Limbs were blown off. Heads were blown off. The sea and the sand were scarlet with blood.

The rattle of machineguns mixed with the boom of artillery, the whump of hand grenades and the wham of exploding shells. Men screamed. They screamed as they were hit, screamed as they crawled through water and sand. They screamed orders. They screamed for their mothers.

The carnage was constant. Men fell dead as they left their landing craft. Others got into the water, only to be shot below the surface by the relentless fire. Those who got to the beach hid behind whatever they could find – and within minutes that included the bodies of fellow soldiers.

It was D-Day. It was the beginning of the end of World War II.

After bringing in divisions from Italy, the Allies attacked southern France in July, leading to the defeat of the German army in France. The local resistance and the Free French Forces liberated Paris on 25 August and the Allies pushed the Germans back in Western Europe during the rest of the year. An attempt to advance into northern Germany spearheaded by an air operation in the Netherlands failed. After that, the Allies slowly pushed into Germany, unsuccessfully trying to cross the Rur River in a large offensive. In Italy the Allied advance also slowed when they ran into the last major German line.

On 22 June, the Soviets launched a strategic offensive in Belarus that resulted in the almost complete destruction of the German Army Group Centre. Soon after that, another Soviet offensive forced German troops out of western Ukraine and eastern Poland. The successful advance of Soviet troops prompted resistance forces in Poland to initiate uprisings. The largest of these, in Warsaw, where German soldiers had massacred 200,000 civilians, and a Slovak uprising in the south, did not get Soviet support and were put down by German forces. The Red Army's offensive in eastern Romania cut off and destroyed the German troops there and triggered successful coups d'etat in Romania and in Bulgaria, followed by those countries' shift to the Allied side.

By September 1944 the Allies had all but defeated Germany. Anglo-American forces closed on the Rhine and territorial losses and bombing by overwhelming Anglo-American attack ended Germany's ability to sustain war for much longer. However, SS coercion and fear of the Allies, especially the Soviets, enabled Hitler to delay the end.

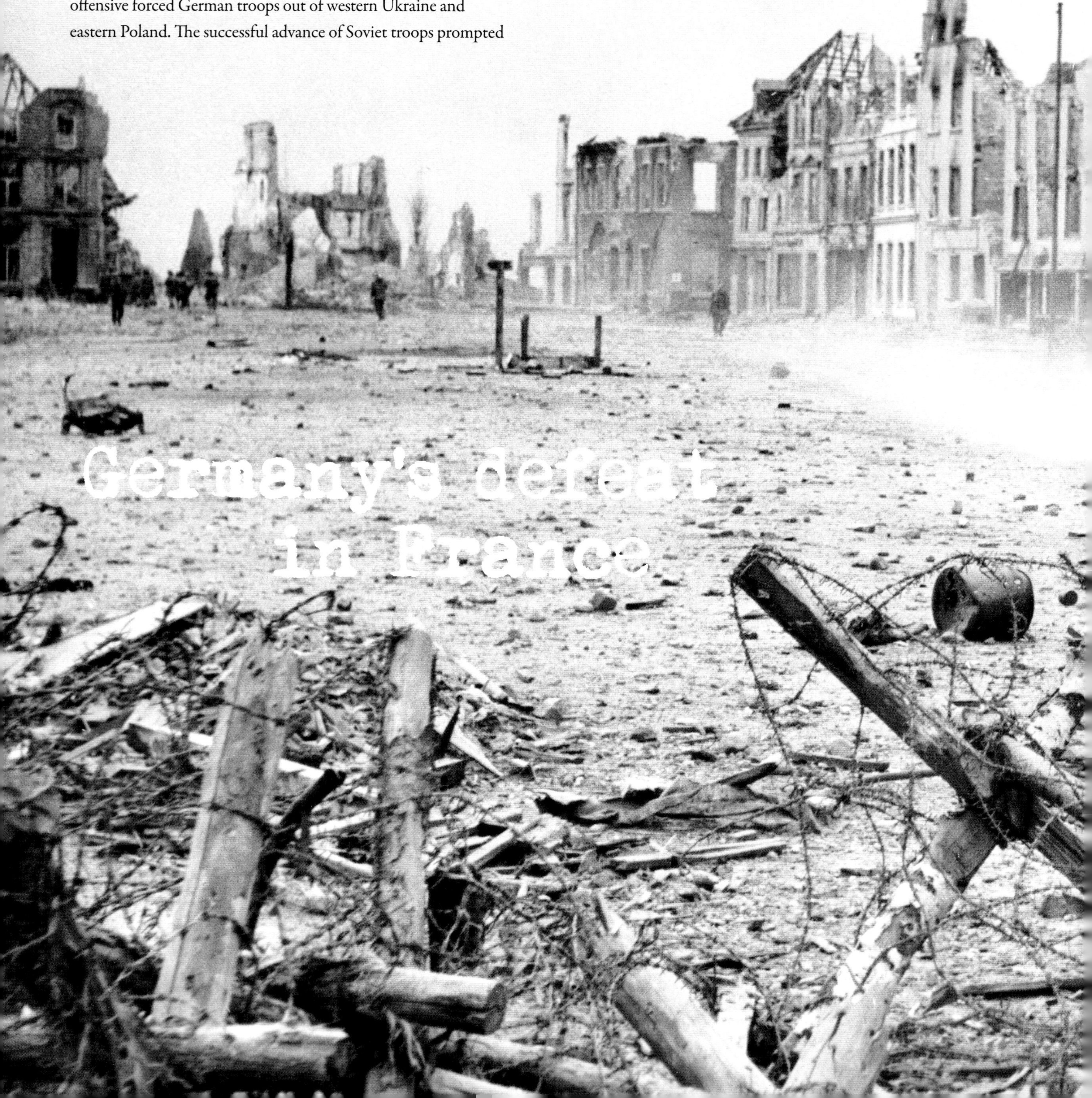

Germany's defeat in France

61

"Honour, eternal honour, to our armies and their leaders. Honour to our nation, which never faltered, even under terrible trials, nor gave in to them. Honour to the united nations, which mingled their blood, their sorrows and their hopes with ours and who today are triumphant with us. Long live France!"

General Charles de Gaulle's broadcast to the French people

VIVE DE GAULLE

Finnish infantry batallion as it begins encircling manoeuvres against German positions in Lapland, Finland, October 1944

In September Red Army troops marched into Yugoslavia and forced the withdrawal of the German Army there, in Greece and in Albania. By this time, the communist partisans under Marshal Josip Broz Tito, who had led an increasingly successful guerrilla campaign against the occupation since 1941, controlled much of Yugoslavia. In northern Serbia, the Red Army, with limited support from Bulgarian forces, helped the partisans in a joint liberation of Belgrade on 20 October. A few days later, the Soviets launched a massive assault against German-occupied Hungary that lasted until the fall of Budapest in February 1945.

In contrast with Soviet victories in the Balkans, the Finnish resistance to the Soviet offensive in the Karelian Isthmus denied the Soviets occupation of Finland and led to the signing of a Soviet-Finnish armistice on relatively mild conditions, with a subsequent shift to the Allied side by Finland.

Last bid

On 16 December 1944, Germany made a last bid for success on the Western Front by using most of its remaining reserves to launch a counter-offensive in the Ardennes to try to split the Allies, encircle them and capture their main supply port at Antwerp to prompt a political settlement. By January, the offensive had been repulsed.

In Italy, the Allies remained stalemated at the German defensive line. In mid-January 1945, the Soviets and Poles attacked in Poland, pushing from the Vistula to the Oder River in Germany, and overran East Prussia.

On 4 February, US, British, and Soviet leaders met for the Yalta Conference. They agreed on the occupation of post-war Germany, and on when the Soviets would join the war against Japan.

"You never really get the smell of burning flesh out of your nose entirely, no matter how long you live."

J.D Salinger

The fighting and killing went on up to the last minute, and even continued into the initial period of supposed peace.

MOHNE DAM
MOHNE DAM

40lb GP
GRAND SLAM
22000lb MC
TALLBOY
12000lb MC
12000lb HC.
8000lb HC.
4000lb MC.
1900lb GP.
2000lb MC
1000lb
MC.
500lb
MC.

RAF Bomber Command helped hasten the end of the war. Relentless mass raids on German cities, while killing thousands of civilians, damaged or destroyed factories crucial to the German war effort. The famous 617 Squadron – the Dam Busters – developed a system that allowed them to drop bombs with great accuracy and the creator of the special dam bombs, Barnes Wallis (left, at his desk), developed two new weapons, the "tallboy" and the "grand slam". The squadron used these to devastating effect, blowing up U-boat pens in Brest and Hamburg, collapsing a vital railway tunnel and several viaducts and bridges, one of which the Germans were using to take oil to the front.

In February the Soviets invaded Silesia and Pomerania, while the Allies entered western Germany and closed the Rhine River. By March, the Allies had crossed the Rhine north and south of the Ruhr, encircling the German Army Group B, while the Soviets advanced to Vienna. In early April, the Allies pushed forward in Italy and swept across western Germany, while Soviet and Polish forces stormed Berlin in late April. The American and Soviet forces linked up on Elbe River on 25 April. On 30 April the Reichstag was captured, marking the military defeat of the Third Reich.

On 12 April, President Roosevelt died and was succeeded by Harry Truman.

"Henceforth the great banner of the freedom of the peoples and peace among peoples will fly over Europe."

Joseph Stalin

Prisoners

DE BLANC
LA GRANDE MAISON DE BLANC

In April the Allies took 1.5 million men prisoner on the Western Front. They also took 120,000 in the last campaign in Italy. In the three or four months to the end of April, more than 800,000 German soldiers surrendered on the Eastern Front. In early April, the first Allied-governed temporary camps were established in western Germany to hold hundreds of thousands of captured or surrendered Axis soldiers. Supreme Headquarters Allied Expeditionary Force (SHAEF) reclassified all prisoners as Disarmed Enemy Forces, not POWs (prisoners of war). This legal fiction circumvented provisions under the Geneva Convention on the treatment of former combatants. By October, thousands had died in the camps from starvation, exposure and disease.

On 25 April 1945, the Finnish Army expelled the last Germans from Finland. They retreated into Norway.

Two days later, as Allied forces closed on Milan, Italian partisans captured dictator Benito Mussolini. It is disputed that he was trying to flee from Italy to Switzerland – he was on the wrong road and was travelling with a German anti-aircraft battalion. On 28 April he was executed in Giulino.

Other Fascists captured with him were taken to Dongo and executed there. The bodies were taken to Milan and hung upside down on the Piazzale Loreto of the city. On 29 April, Rodolfo Graziani surrendered all Fascist Italian armed forces at Caserta.

German forces surrendered in Italy on 29 April. On 7 May they signed an unconditional surrender. German Army Group Centre resisted in Prague until 11 May.

Hitler's suicide

On 30 April, as the Battle of Berlin raged above him, realising that all was lost and not wanting to suffer Mussolini's fate, Hitler committed suicide in his bunker with his new wife, Eva Braun. In his will, he dismissed Hermann Goering and Interior Minister Heinrich Himmler after each had tried to seize control of the crumbling Third Reich. Hitler appointed Admiral Karl Doenitz as the "President of Germany" and Joseph Goebbels as the new Chancellor. However, Goebbels committed suicide next day, leaving Doenitz as leader.

On 29 April, the day before Hitler died, SS General Karl Wolff signed a surrender document at Caserta on behalf of General Heinrich von Vietinghoff, after prolonged unauthorised secret negotiations with the Allies, which were viewed with suspicion by the Soviet Union as trying to reach a separate peace. Wolff agreed to a ceasefire and surrender of all forces under the command of Vietinghoff at 2pm on 2 May. Accordingly, after wrangling between Wolff and Albert Kesselring in the early hours of 2 May, nearly a million men in Italy and Austria surrendered unconditionally to British General Harold Alexander at 2pm.

The Battle of Berlin ended on 2 May when the commander of the Berlin defence area, General Helmuth Weidling, unconditionally surrendered the city to Soviet General Vasily Chuikov. On the same day the officers commanding the two armies of Army Group Vistula north of Berlin surrendered. The date is also believed to be the day Hitler's deputy, Martin Bormann died, according to Artur Axmann, who said he saw Bormann die near Lehrter railway station after encountering a Red Army patrol. The station is close to where the remains of Bormann, confirmed as his by a DNA test in 1998, were unearthed on 7 December 1972.

Surrender

"If we have power, we'll never give it up unless we are carried out of our offices as corpses."

Joseph Goebbels

"Our losses have reached an intolerable level."

Karl Doenitz

On 4 May 1945, Field Marshal Bernard Montgomery took the unconditional military surrender from Admiral Hans-Georg von Friedeburg, and General Eberhard Kinzel, of all German forces "in Holland, in northwest Germany including the Frisian Islands and Heligoland and all other islands, in Schleswig-Holstein, and in Denmark… includ[ing] all naval ships in these areas". This meant the surrender of a million men. On 5 May, Doenitz ordered all U-boats to cease offensive operations and return to their bases.

On 5 May the Czech resistance started the Prague Uprising. The next day, the Soviets launched the Prague Offensive, the last major Soviet operation of the war. The offensive, and the battle for Prague, was fought on the Eastern Front from 6 May to 11 May. It is noteworthy in that it ended after the Third Reich capitulated on 8 May and that it was fought at the same time as the Prague Uprising.

Prague was eventually captured by the USSR.

On 6 May, Nazi leader and Hitler's second-in-command Hermann Goering surrendered, with his wife and daughter at the Germany-Austria border. He was the most powerful Nazi official still alive.

At 10am on 8 May, the Channel islanders were told by the German authorities that the war was over. Churchill made a radio broadcast at 3pm during which he announced: "Hostilities will end officially at one minute after midnight tonight, but in the interests of saving lives the ceasefire began yesterday to be sounded all along the front, and our dear Channel Islands are also to be freed today."

Thirty minutes after the fall of Breslau on 6 May, the Chief of Staff of the German Armed Forces High Command, General Alfred Jodl, arrived in Reims and, following Doenitz's instructions, offered to surrender all forces. This was the same negotiating position von Friedeburg had made to Montgomery, and like Montgomery, the Supreme Allied Commander, General Dwight Eisenhower, threatened to break off all negotiations unless the Germans agreed to a complete unconditional surrender. Eisenhower explicitly told Jodl that he would order western lines closed to German soldiers, thus forcing them to surrender to the Soviets. Jodl sent a signal to Doenitz telling him of Eisenhower's declaration. Just after midnight, Doenitz, accepting the inevitable, sent a signal to Jodl authorising the complete and total surrender of all German forces.

At 2.41am on 7 May, at SHAEF headquarters in Reims, Jodl signed the unconditional surrender document for all German forces. It included the phrase "All forces under German control to cease active operations at 2301 hours Central European Time on May 8, 1945." That day General Franz Boehme announced the unconditional surrender of German troops in Norway. Next day, Field Marshal Wilhelm Keitel and other German Supreme Command representatives went to Berlin, and just before midnight signed a similar document, explicitly surrendering to Soviet forces, in the presence of General Georgi Zhukov. The signing ceremony took place in a former German Army engineering school in the Berlin district of Karlshorst.

News of the imminent surrender broke in the West on 8 May and celebrations erupted throughout Europe. In the US, Americans awoke to the news and declared 8 May VE Day.

Although most German forces obeyed the order to surrender, not all did so. The largest contingent was Army Group Centre under the command of Field Marshal Ferdinand Schoerner, who had been promoted to Commander-in-Chief of the Army on 30 April in Hitler's will. On 8 May, Schoerner deserted his command and flew to Austria. The Soviet Army sent an overwhelming force against Army Group Centre in the Prague Offensive, forcing it to capitulate by 11 May. Other forces which did not surrender on 8 May surrendered piecemeal.

On 13 May, the Red Army halted all offensives in Europe. Isolated pockets of resistance in Czechoslovakia were mopped up by this date. The garrison on Alderney, one of the occupied Channel Islands, surrendered on 16 May, a week after the garrisons on the other Channel Islands, which surrendered on 9 May.

The Georgian Uprising of Texel (5 April–20 May) was Europe's last battle in World War II. It was fought between Georgian Nazi collaborators on the Dutch island of Texel and its German occupiers.

A small group of German soldiers was abandoned on Bear Island, halfway between northernmost Norway and Greenland. They were supposed to establish and man a weather station there, but after losing radio contact in May 1945 they were isolated, and surrendered to Norwegian seal hunters on 4 September.

Karl Doenitz continued to act as if he were the German head of state, but his Flensburg government (so-called because it was based at Flensburg in northern Germany and controlled only a small area around the town), was not recognised by the Allies. On 12 May an Allied team arrived in Flensburg and soon realised there was no need to act through the Flensburg government and that its members should be arrested. On 23 May, acting on SHAEF's orders and with the approval of the Soviets, American Major General Lowell Rooks summoned Doenitz and told him that he and the rest of his government were under arrest and that their government was dissolved.

The Allies realised that although the German armed forces had surrendered unconditionally, SHAEF had failed to use the document created by the European Advisory Commission, so there had been no formal surrender by the civilian German government. This was considered important because just as the civilian, but not military, surrender in 1918 had been used by Hitler to create the "stab in the back" argument, the Allies did not want to give any future hostile German regime a legal argument to resurrect an old quarrel.

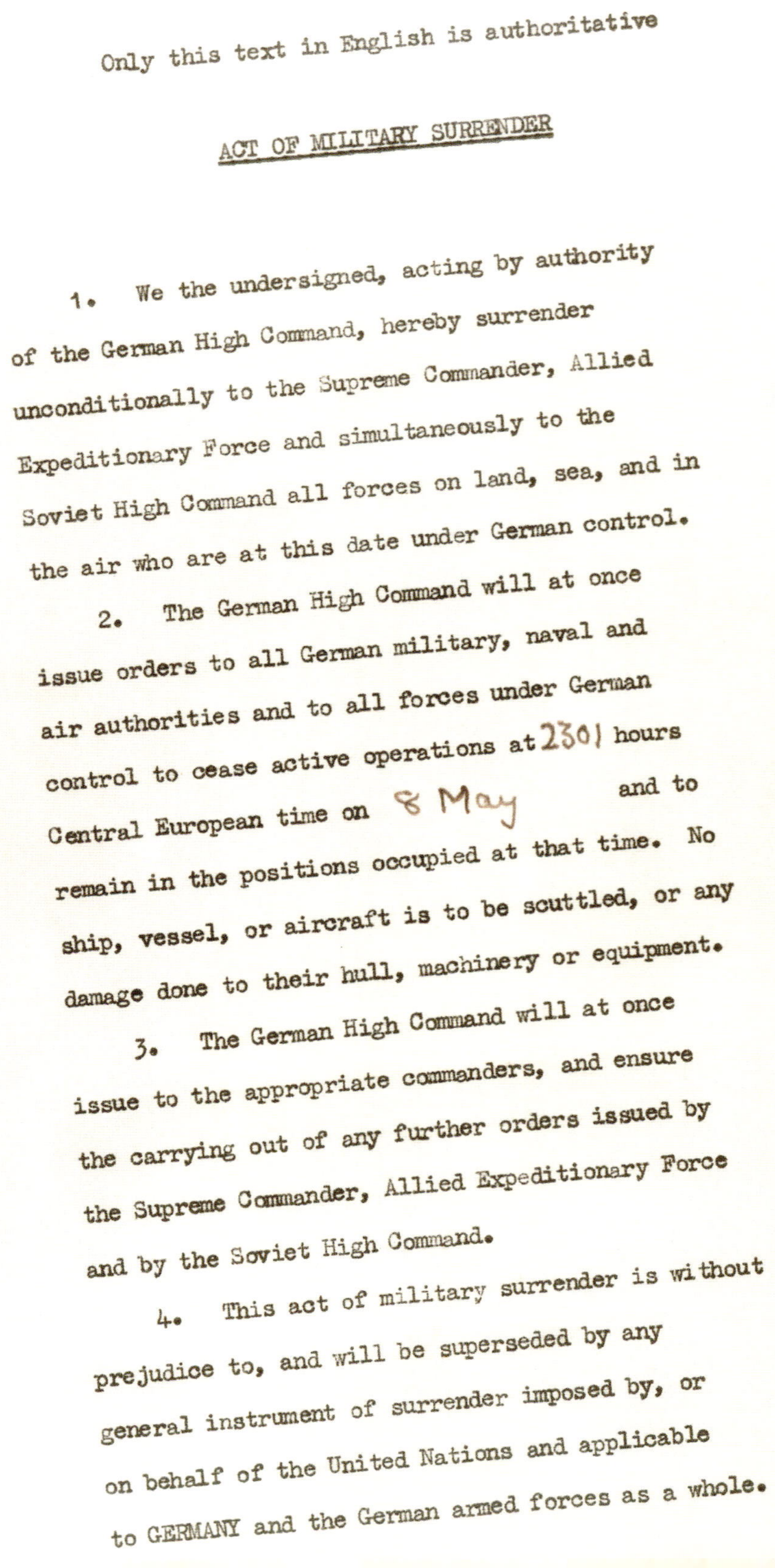

Only this text in English is authoritative

ACT OF MILITARY SURRENDER

1. We the undersigned, acting by authority of the German High Command, hereby surrender unconditionally to the Supreme Commander, Allied Expeditionary Force and simultaneously to the Soviet High Command all forces on land, sea, and in the air who are at this date under German control.

2. The German High Command will at once issue orders to all German military, naval and air authorities and to all forces under German control to cease active operations at 2301 hours Central European time on 8 May and to remain in the positions occupied at that time. No ship, vessel, or aircraft is to be scuttled, or any damage done to their hull, machinery or equipment.

3. The German High Command will at once issue to the appropriate commanders, and ensure the carrying out of any further orders issued by the Supreme Commander, Allied Expeditionary Force and by the Soviet High Command.

4. This act of military surrender is without prejudice to, and will be superseded by any general instrument of surrender imposed by, or on behalf of the United Nations and applicable to GERMANY and the German armed forces as a whole.

The Declaration Regarding the Defeat of Germany and the Assumption of Supreme Authority by Allied Powers was signed by the Allies on 5 June. It included this:

"The Governments of the United States of America, the Union of Soviet Socialist Republics, the United Kingdom and the Provisional Government of the French Republic, hereby assume supreme authority with respect to Germany, including all the powers possessed by the German Government, the High Command and any state, municipal, or local government or authority. The assumption, for the purposes stated above, of the said authority and powers does not effect the annexation of Germany. —US Department of State, Treaties and Other International Acts Series, No. 1520."

It is disputed whether this assumption of power constituted debellation – the end of a war caused by the complete destruction of a hostile state.

Cessation of hostilities between the United States and Germany was officially proclaimed on 13 December 1946 by President Truman.

5. In the event of the German High Command or any of the forces under their control failing to act in accordance with this Act of Surrender, the Supreme Commander, Allied Expeditionary Force and the Soviet High Command will take such punitive or other action as they deem appropriate.

Signed at Rheims, France at 0241 on the 7th day of May, 1945.

On behalf of the German High Command.

IN THE PRESENCE OF

On behalf of the Supreme Commander, Allied Expeditionary Force.

On behalf of the Soviet High Command.

-2-

Potsdam

"The alternative for Japan is prompt and utter destruction."

Potsdam statement

On 11 July, Allied leaders met in Potsdam, Germany. They confirmed agreements about Germany and repeated the demand for unconditional surrender of all Japanese forces, specifically saying that "the alternative for Japan is prompt and utter destruction". During this conference Britain held its general election, and Clement Attlee replaced Churchill as Prime Minister.

As Japan continued to ignore the Potsdam terms, the US dropped atomic bombs on Hiroshima and Nagasaki on 6 and 9 August. The US and its allies justified the bombings as necessary to avoid invading the Japanese home islands, which would cost the lives of 250,000–500,000 Allied troops and millions of Japanese troops and civilians. Between the two bombings, the Soviets invaded Japanese-held Manchuria, and quickly defeated the Kwantung Army, the largest Japanese fighting force.

On 15 August 1945 Japan surrendered, with the documents signed aboard the battleship USS *Missouri* on 2 September 1945.

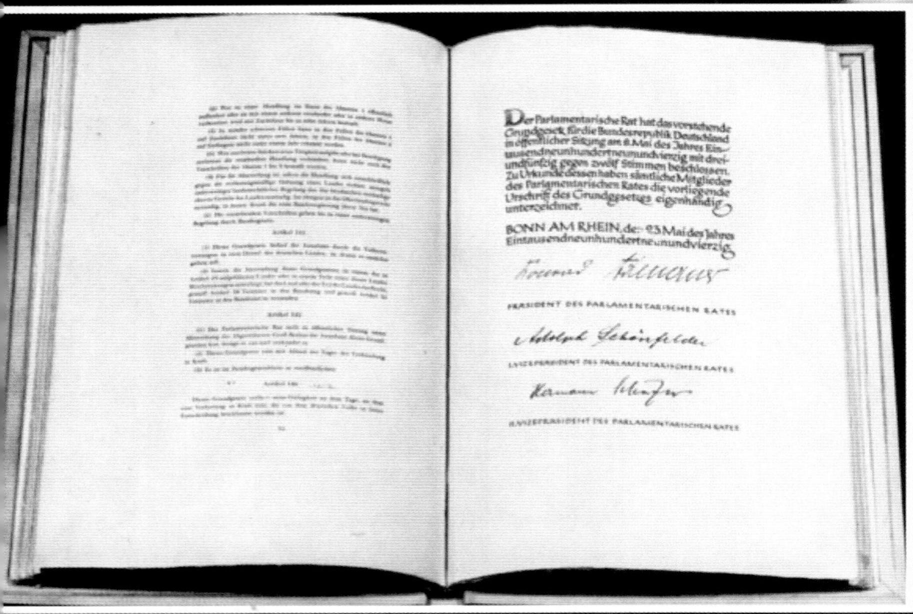

“Humility must be the measure of a man whose success was bought with the blood of his subordinates, and paid for with the lives of his friends.”

Dwight Eisenhower

Peace conference

The Paris Peace Conference ended on 10 February 1947 with the signing of peace treaties by the Allies with the minor European Axis powers (Italy, Romania, Hungary, Bulgaria, and Finland).

The Federal Republic of Germany, founded on 23 May 1949, formed its first government on 20 September 1949. The German Democratic Republic was formed on 7 October.

The formal end of a state of war with Germany was declared by many former Allies in 1950. In the Petersberg Agreement of 22 November 1949, it was noted that the West German government wanted an end to the state of war, but the request could not be granted. The US state of war with Germany was being maintained for legal reasons, and though it was softened somewhat it was not suspended because "the US wants to retain a legal basis for keeping a US force in Western Germany". At a meeting of the Foreign Ministers of France, the UK and the US in New York from 12 September to 19 December 1950, it was stated that among other measures to strengthen West Germany's position in the Cold War the Allies would "end by legislation the state of war with Germany". In 1951, many former Allies did end their state of war with Germany: Australia, South Africa, Britain, Canada, Italy, New Zealand, the Netherlands and the United States. The state of war between Germany and the Soviet Union was ended in early 1955.

Concentration camps and refugees

In the last months of the war and immediately afterwards, Allied soldiers discovered concentration camps used by the Nazis to imprison and kill an estimated 11 million people, six million of whom were Jews. The remaining five million were Romanis, Slavs, homosexuals and various minorities and disabled people, as well as political enemies of the Nazi regime (particularly communists). The best-known of these is the death camp at Auschwitz in which 1.1-1.6 million Jews and political prisoners were killed.

LOS ESPANOLES ANTIFASCISTAS
SALUDAN A LAS FUERZAS

Celebrations

PEACE
NO WAITING
TUESDAYS
THURSDAYS
SATURDAYS

EXTRA | PARIS EDITION THE STARS AND STRIPES | EXTRA

Daily Newspaper of U.S. Armed Forces in the European Theater of Operations

Vol. 1—No. 285 | 1 Fr. | Tuesday, May 8, 1945

VICTORY

Nazis Reveal Surrender To Western Allies, Russia

The unconditional surrender of Germany to the Western Allies and Soviet Russia was announced by the German high command yesterday morning.

The official announcements from the Allied governments are expected to come simultaneously from Washington, London and Moscow today.

The British Ministry of Information, proclaiming that today would be 'Victory in Europe Day,' said Prime Minister Churchill would make 'an official announcement' at 3 PM.

President Truman said he had agreed with the British and Russian governments that no surrender proclamation would be made 'until simultaneous announcement ... made by the three governments.'

... a cablegram last night ... his armies on

Individuals reacted differently to the end of the nightmare: some celebrated by partying; others spent the day in quiet reflection; and some were too busy to do either. Ultimately nothing would be the same again.

The end of World War I on 11 November 1918 shocked many soldiers and civilians because the German collapse was so sudden. By contrast, it was clear – since at least the start of 1945 – that the end of World War II in Europe was in sight.

The fighting and killing went on up to the last minute, and even continued into the initial period of supposed peace. A German U-boat sank two merchant ships on 7 May off the Scottish coast, and some Germans continued to fight against the Red Army for several days after VE Day.

A common reaction to the news of peace among soldiers in Europe was "I've survived". Stuart Hills, a British officer with an armoured regiment, finished the war deep in Germany. On hearing the news he felt immediate exhilaration and marked the occasion with some "liberated" champagne. But then reaction set in as he thought of his friends who had been killed, and he no longer felt like celebrating.

A Scottish battalion let off some flares when the news came through. Later, rum was issued and one platoon held a sing-song. Otherwise, VE Day passed without incident. For this unit, still close to German forces that refused to believe the war was over, it was business as usual.

The 8th Hussars (part of 7th Armoured Division, also known as the Desert Rats) celebrated VE Day in northern Germany with a church parade followed by rum punch drunk beside bonfires on which swastikas were ceremonially burned.

Elsewhere there were wilder celebrations, with men going absent without leave and even some alcohol-fuelled deaths, but these happened farther back from the front line.

In general terms, the British army remained disciplined. The fighting was over, but surrounded by a near-starving civilian population eking a living in the ruins of Germany's towns and cities, everyone could see there was still much to do. Moreover, the Far East was in the back of many minds.

For the Allies, the conflict in Europe was only half the war. At that stage, the atomic bomb was a secret known to few, and the end of the war with Japan seemed a long way off.

* Desert Rats were 7th Arm. Div. not the Hussars

"Our dear Channel Islands are also to be freed today."

Winston Churchill

Many men in the European theatre expected to be sent to fight the Japanese in Burma, Malaya and the Pacific. The men of the British Liberation Army serving in Germany interpreted the initials BLA as "Burma Looms Ahead".

Not surprisingly, for some troops in Burma or sailors of the British Pacific Fleet fighting beside the US Navy, the news of victory in Europe seemed somehow unreal. As if to rub home that there was still a war, the aircraft carrier HMS *Victorious* was hit by a kamikaze plane the day after VE Day.

Troops out of the line in the Far East could celebrate. Some got alcohol, while the Women's Auxiliary Service (Burma), attached to the 26th Indian Division, supplied mugs of tea to a beach race meeting. A surprising number of soldiers who served in Burma did not even mention VE Day in their memoirs and diaries.

One group who did hear the news from Europe were prisoners of war still in terrible conditions in Changi Jail, Singapore, who picked up Churchill's victory broadcast on clandestine radios.

Many sailors of the Royal Navy discovered the news of VE Day through their ships' radio operators as they picked up BBC broadcasts. Many captains celebrated by "splicing the mainbrace" – issuing a rum ration.

For some, it was a pleasant interlude in a normal working day. A force of British and Canadian ships spent VE Day sailing to Jersey and Guernsey, occupied since 1940. Although in his victory broadcast Churchill had announced that "our dear Channel Islands are also to be freed today", it was unclear whether the occupying force intended to fight or surrender. But the liberation was achieved peacefully, with the Bailiff of Jersey leading the crowds in St Helier in singing the National Anthem, which the Germans had banned during the war.

Britain

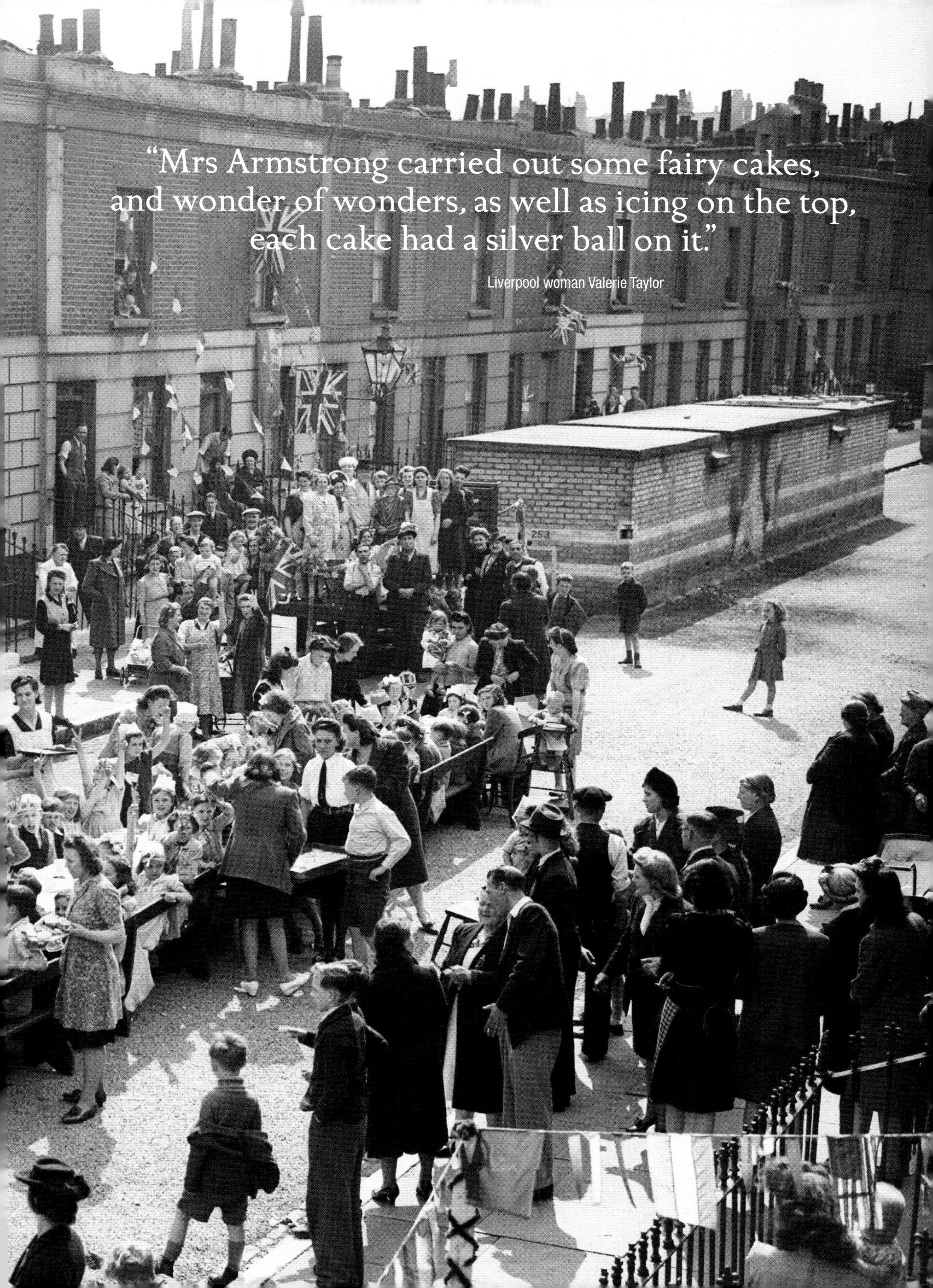

“Mrs Armstrong carried out some fairy cakes, and wonder of wonders, as well as icing on the top, each cake had a silver ball on it.”

Liverpool woman Valerie Taylor

In much of Britain, VE Day was marked by street parties. The people badly needed to let their hair down. The country was war-weary by May 1945.

As was the way of things in Britain, the Home Office issued a circular telling people how they could celebrate: "Bonfires will be allowed, but the government trusts that only material with no salvage value will be used."

The Board of Trade did the same: "Until the end of May you may buy cotton bunting without coupons, as long as it is red, white or blue, and does not cost more than one shilling and three pence a square yard."

Half a million homes had been destroyed and many millions of lives disrupted. Although the casualty lists from the battlefields were lower than in World War I, they were still terrible.

People were already on the streets celebrating on 7 May and huge crowds gathered in London next day.

At 1pm Churchill went to Buckingham Palace to have a celebratory lunch with King George.

POST OFFICE
BUS STOP
WESTER
UNION
CABLEGRA

"When the crowd saw Churchill there was a deep, full-throated, almost reverent roar."

Author Molly Panter-Downs

At 3pm he spoke to the nation from the Cabinet Room at 10 Downing Street. In Trafalgar Square, a witness noted, "there was an extraordinary hush over the assembled multitude" as Churchill's voice was relayed over loudspeakers: "Yesterday morning at 2.41am at headquarters, General Jodl, the representative of the German High Command, and Grand Admiral Doenitz, the designated head of the German State, signed the act of unconditional surrender of all German land, sea and air forces in Europe to the Allied Expeditionary Force, and simultaneously to the Soviet High Command." He reminded people that Japan had still to be defeated, but that the people of Great Britain "may allow ourselves a brief period of rejoicing. Advance Britannia. Long live the cause of freedom! God save the King!"

Three Lancasters flew over London and dropped red and green flares. About 50,000 people gathered between Trafalgar Square and Big Ben.

Winston Churchill's speech to VE Day crowds at Whitehall

My dear friends, this is your hour. This is not victory of a party or of any class. It's a victory of the great British nation as a whole. We were the first, in this ancient island, to draw the sword against tyranny. After a while we were left all alone against the most tremendous military power that has been seen. We were all alone for a whole year.

There we stood, alone. Did anyone want to give in? [The crowd shouted "No."] Were we down-hearted? ["No!"] The lights went out and the bombs came down. But every man, woman and child in the country had no thought of quitting the struggle. London can take it. So we came back after long months from the jaws of death, out of the mouth of hell, while all the world wondered. When shall the reputation and faith of this generation of English men and women fail? I say that in the long years to come not only will the people of this island but of the world, wherever the bird of freedom chirps in human hearts, look back to what we've done and they will say "do not despair, do not yield to violence and tyranny, march straight forward and die if need be-unconquered." Now we have emerged from one deadly struggle – a terrible foe has been cast on the ground and awaits our judgment and our mercy.

But there is another foe who occupies large portions of the British Empire, a foe stained with cruelty and greed – the Japanese. I rejoice we can all take a night off today and another day tomorrow. Tomorrow our great Russian allies will also be celebrating victory and after that we must begin the task of rebuilding our hearth and homes, doing our utmost to make this country a land in which all have a chance, in which all have a duty, and we must turn ourselves to fulfil our duty to our own countrymen, and to our gallant allies of the United States who were so foully and treacherously attacked by Japan. We will go hand in hand with them. Even if it is a hard struggle we will not be the ones who fail.

After the broadcast Churchill went to Parliament to address the Commons. He then led some MPs to a thanksgiving service. At 5.30pm, the doors to the Buckingham Palace balcony opened. Out walked the King and Queen and their two girls, Princesses Elizabeth and Margaret. Beside them was the man of the hour himself, Churchill. They smiled and waved to the crowds, who cheered and shouted "God Save the King and Queen". Author Mollie Panter-Downes later wrote of the moment in the *New Yorker*: "Thousands of King George's subjects wedged themselves in front of the Palace throughout the day, chanting ceaselessly 'We want the King' and cheering themselves hoarse when he and the Queen and their daughters appeared, but when the crowd saw Churchill there was a deep, full-throated, almost reverent roar."

Later in the evening the King and the Queen appeared again to much cheering and well-wishes from below. Unknown to the crowds, however, was that this was not just for their benefit.

Eager to experience the crowds, the two princesses had managed to persuade their parents to let them outside the palace grounds for a while. Elizabeth and Margaret walked around Green Park and joined the throng outside the front gates. In the celebrations, most people wouldn't have thought much of two girls happily walking around, let alone that one of them was their future queen. The girls were able to stay incognito and get a real sense of what the ordinary British citizen was feeling.

Elizabeth later admitted she and Margaret had sent word back to the Palace that they were out the front and waiting for their

parents to appear. “My sister and I realised we couldn’t see what the crowds were enjoying ... so we asked my parents if we could go out and see for ourselves ... After crossing Green Park we stood outside and shouted, ‘We want the King’, and were successful in seeing my parents on the balcony, having cheated slightly because we sent a message into the house to say we were waiting outside. I think it was one of the more memorable nights of my life.”

Elsewhere the evening turned into a citywide party. Mollie Panter-Downes recalled the atmosphere: “American sailors and laughing girls formed a conga line down the middle of Piccadilly and cockneys linked arms in the Lambeth Walk. The most tolerant, self-effacing people in London on VE Day were the police, who simply stood by, smiling benignly, while soldiers swung by one arm from the lamp standards and laughing groups tore down hoardings to build the evening’s bonfires.”

Street parties were organised across the land and neighbours pooled food, much of which was still rationed.

All over the country people held fancy dress parades for children, got drunk, made a din, sang and danced in the streets and went to church to give thanks to God for victory.

For all too many people, mourning a loved one killed in service or in a German air raid, the moment of victory was bittersweet. For others, after the parties were over, there was a sense of anti-climax.

The last official event of VE Day was a broadcast to the nation by the King at 9pm.

An excerpt of King George VI's radio address to the nation on VE Day

Today we give thanks to Almighty God for a great deliverance. Speaking from our Empire's oldest capital city, war-battered but never for on moment daunted or dismayed – speaking from London, I ask you to join with me in that act of thanksgiving.

Germany, the enemy who drove all Europe into war, has been finally overcome. In the Far East we have yet to deal with the Japanese, a determined and cruel foe. To this we shall turn with the utmost resolve and with all our resources. But at this hour, when the dreadful shadow of war has passed far from our hearths and homes in these islands, we may at last make one pause for thanksgiving and then turn our thoughts to the tasks all over the world which peace in Europe brings with it.

Let us remember those who will not come back: their constancy and courage in battle, their sacrifice and endurance in the face of a merciless enemy; let us remember the men in all the services, and the women in all the services, who have laid down their lives. We have come to the end of our tribulation and they are not with us at the moment of our rejoicing.

Then let us salute in proud gratitude the great host of the living who have brought us to victory. I cannot praise them to the measure of each one's service, for in a total war, the efforts of all rise to the same noble height, and all are devoted to the common purpose.

Armed or unarmed, men and women, you have fought and striven and endured to your utmost. No one knows that better than I do, and as your King, I thank with a full heart those who bore arms so valiantly on land and sea, or in the air, and all civilians who, shouldering their many burdens, have carried them unflinchingly without complaint.

Buckingham Palace was lit by floodlights for the first time since 1939 and two searchlights made a giant V above St Paul's Cathedral. It was a symbolic gesture for a city that had spent years in blackout. People built street fires out of whatever flammable materials they could find. Witnesses reported that London had the same red glow as during the Blitz – but this time it was in celebration. Some fires got out of hand and the London Fire Brigade had to be called – something they were very experienced at. People let off fireworks – prohibited during the war – to give the celebrations colour.

World War II diarist Nella Last recorded the scene in her diary: "All the shops had got their rosettes and tri-coloured button-holes in the windows and men putting up lengths of little pennants and flags. Till at three o'clock, the Germans announced it was all over. As if by magic, long ladders appeared, for putting up flags and streamers. A complete stranger to the situation could have felt the tenseness and feeling of expectation. Like myself, Steve [Howson, a wartime friend] has a real fear of Russia. He thinks in, say, 20 years or so, when Nazism has finally gone, Germany and not Russia will be our Allies."

The police reported that there was almost no criminal activity during the day despite the boisterous behaviour of tens of thousands. In the early hours of 9 May the illuminations in London were turned off. The war in Japan was still being fought and austerity had become normal for many people. But for one short day people could let their hair down.

There had been years of austerity and rationing: five inches of water for a bath, few eggs, no bananas and the motto "make do and mend". Half a million homes had been destroyed, thousands of civilians had been killed and many millions of lives disrupted. And although the casualty lists from the battlefields were lower than in World War I, they were still terrible.

Liverpool

Celebrations were not confined to the capital. Throughout the country people had huddled around any radio they could find to hear Churchill's announcement. Those who missed it heard the news from others or read it in the evening newspapers.

Mary was 18 in 1945, and remembers when the news swept through Liverpool: "There was much for us to be happy about and people danced in the streets and the pubs stayed open all day long. The news of the capitulation came through very late at night when most people were asleep. But they were soon woken up and once again there was dancing in the streets. A lot of people were still in their nightclothes, and once again the pub doors were opened. I'm afraid I missed out on this night because I had to get up early for work the following morning."

People in Liverpool organised street parties. In the months leading up to 8 May, once victory in Europe started to appear more likely, households saved rations for the celebrations that would follow.

To a seven-year-old such as Valerie Taylor, the sort of food prepared that day was almost unheard of after years of rationing: "Then the tablecloths were laid and lastly the food was brought out, sandwiches and jellies, and then Mrs Armstrong carried out some fairy cakes, and wonder of wonders, as well as icing on the top, each cake had a silver ball on it."

The day had an extra significance for Margaret Brook, who was turning six on 8 May. She lived on Colville Street in Liverpool: "On the evening of May 7, as their husbands set up trestle tables down the centre of the street, all the women sat in small groups on the pavement outside their houses, pleased with what they had achieved; and hopeful that the weather would hold fine for the following day, VE Day. It was a holiday, workers had taken the day off, banks libraries and schools were closed, the whole country was about to celebrate the end of six long years of war."

Manchester

In Manchester, the celebrations mirrored those in London. As night fell, the central streets were crowded. Albert Square, in the heart of the city, was transformed into a dance floor. Strangers danced together. Music played through loudspeakers at the town hall.

A Manchester Guardian report of the evening told of young people climbing on the roofs of air-raid shelters to dance. The paper suggested sailors had started it, but in any case they were soon followed by more, especially the women of the Women's Auxiliary Air Force and Auxiliary Territorial Service.

Occasionally the dark sky lit up in bright colours as fireworks were noisily set off.

Many in the crowds were handed paper hats, streamers, confetti and other carnival accessories. It was odd after years of paper being scarce that such items were suddenly everywhere.

Gloria Sutcliffe was 15 when she and her sister caught the bus into Manchester that night to take part: "I could not believe my eyes! There were simply thousands of people stretching before me until they disappeared out of Albert Square.

"The view was amazing. Flags of all different colours and sizes, service hats of every description held aloft on sticks and umbrellas with numerous ones suddenly being thrown high into the air over their owners' heads. And the singing! It came from every direction, rising to great crescendos in places, starting or overlapping in others. *Run Rabbit*, *White Cliffs of Dover*, *It's a Long Way to Tipperary* and countless other war-time favourites filled the air all around. With *Rule Britannia* rising from the group closest to us, the whole scene was simply and unbelievably magic to me then.

"Everyone greeted and danced with those next to them, although in reality most would never have met before their arrival in the crowd. It was as if one gigantic family from all over the world had gathered to celebrate a universal family event."

Glasgow

Scotland also celebrated enthusiastically. Tommy Mac was 14, and later remembered how Glasgow responded to Churchill's broadcast: "The entire city went a little mad. Schools were closed for the day. It was a day of celebration!"

Having found a girl to go with him, Tommy watched the party down Hope Street as they made their way to George Square, the focal point of the celebrations: "The tram cars in Hope Street were filled with servicemen of all nationalities – American, Canadian, Australian, European; all of them commandeering the trams and singing and dancing up and down the length of Hope Street, singing all kinds of songs I had never heard before.

"At the bottom of the street the dance was the eightsome reel – this of course took precedence over all the other carousing. This was Scotland's national dance, and everyone could join in. The music was relayed from the old Kemsley House, former home of the Glasgow *Daily Record*, who also supplied the lighting for the parade. To see the lights go on again was a miracle in itself.

"I didn't see too many drunks, now that I think on it. There was no need. The spirits were lifted high enough as it was. It was quite wonderful to see all the men and women in uniform hugging, kissing and generally flirting with the civilian population."

The tension throughout Britain of six long years was suddenly relaxed. Some found they had lost a sense of purpose in their lives, a feeling made worse by the austerity. The war had been won, but the peace did not promise to be easy.

Paris

"The people of Paris responded with a full-throated yell and the bedlam of every auto horn in the city."

Yank magazine

General Charles de Gaulle's broadcast to the French people

The war has been won. This is victory. It is the victory of the united nations and that of France. The German enemy has surrendered to the Allied armies in the west and east. The French High Command was present and a party to the act of capitulation.

In the state of disorganisation of the German public authorities and command it is possible that certain enemy groups may intend here and there to prolong on their own account a senseless resistance. But Germany is beaten and has signed her disaster.

While the rays of glory once again lend brilliance to our flags, the country turns its thoughts and affection first of all toward those who died for her and then toward those who in her service struggled and suffered so much. Not one single act of courage or self-sacrifice of her sons and daughters, not one single hardship of her captive men and women, not one single bereavement and sacrifice, not one single tear, will have been wasted in vain.

In the national rejoicing and pride, the French people send brotherly greetings to their gallant Allies, who, like themselves and for the same cause, have sustained so many hardships over such a long period, to their heroic armies and to those commanding them, and to all those men and women who, throughout the world, fought, suffered and worked so that the cause of liberty and justice might ultimately prevail.

Honour, eternal honour, to our armies and their leaders. Honour to our nation, which never faltered, even under terrible trials, nor gave in to them. Honour to the united nations, which mingled their blood, their sorrows and their hopes with ours and who today are triumphant with us.

Long live France!

Parisians were overjoyed at the news of Germany's defeat. The city, like the rest of France, had fallen early in the war and suffered the humiliation of Nazi occupation. But the French Resistance had fought back and, with the help of the Allies, had won. And now it was the Germans' turn to surrender. The sweet feeling of revenge lingered in the air on 8 May 1945.

The liberation of Paris started on 19 August 1944 and lasted six days. The uprising began with the French Resistance attacking the German garrison. They received reinforcements from the Free French Army of Liberation and the US Army under General George Patton.

On 8 May 1945, the mood among Parisians when the news came through that the Germans had surrendered almost matched the mood when the city had been freed 10 months earlier.

General Charles de Gaulle, the war hero and Provisional President of the Free French Republic, made the announcement at 3pm.

Yank magazine correspondents Allan Ecker and Howard Katzender followed the day's events: "It was a long way even the few blocks from Fouqet's restaurant to the Arc de Triomphe if you tried to

walk up the Champs on VE Day in Paris. From one side of the broad and beautiful avenue to the other, all the way from the Obelisk in the Place de la Concorde to the Arc de Triomphe in the Place d'Etoile, there was hardly any place to breathe and no place at all to move.

"Air raid sirens, so long a symbol of terror to the French and to all the war-torn world, this time sounded a message of freedom. And the people of Paris responded with a full-throated yell and the bedlam of every auto horn in the city.

"At Marbeuf on the Champs Elysees, a huge throng of students formed a circle on the lawn and sang the stirring French songs, the Marseillaise, the Internationale, the Madelon and the great marching songs of many wars.

"All day long the aircraft of the Allies buzzed the Champs Elysees, swooping down to tree-top level, then zooming up to clear the Arc de Triomphe."

The only people working were the proprietors of footpath cafes and hawkers of flags and souvenirs. Newspaper stallholders sold out 20 different papers in no time – and continued selling as fresh extras kept rolling off the presses.

LUNCH DEP

United States

In the US, President Truman, who turned 61 that day, dedicated the victory to the memory of his predecessor, Franklin Roosevelt, who had died on 12 April. Flags stayed at half-mast for the rest of the 30-day mourning period.

Massive celebrations took place in New York, Chicago, Los Angeles and Miami. The *New York Times* reported:

"New York City's millions reacted in two sharply contrasting ways yesterday to the news of the unconditional surrender of the German armies. A large and noisy minority greeted it with the turbulent enthusiasm of New Year's Eve and Election Night rolled into one. However, the great bulk of the city's population responded with quiet thanksgiving that the war in Europe was won, tempered by the realization that a grim and bitter struggle still was ahead in the Pacific and the fact that the nation is still in mourning for its fallen President and Commander in Chief.

"Times Square, the financial section and the garment district were thronged from mid-morning on with wildly jubilant celebrators who tooted horns, staged impromptu parades and filled the canyons between the skyscrapers with fluttering scraps of paper. Elsewhere in the metropolitan area, however, war plants continued to hum, schools, offices and factories carried on their normal activities, and residential areas were calmly joyful.

"One factor that helped to dampen the celebration was the bewilderment of large segments of the population at the absence of an official proclamation to back up the news contained in flaring headlines and radio bulletins. With the premature rumor of ten days ago fresh in everyone's mind, and millions still mindful of the false armistice of 1918, there was widespread skepticism over the authenticity of the news.

"By mid-afternoon loudspeakers were blaring into the ears of the exulting thousands in the amusement district the news that President Truman's proclamation was being held up by the necessity of coordinating it with the announcements from London and Moscow, and that the formal celebration of the long-awaited VE Day would be delayed until today.

"This sobering note gradually calmed the wild demonstration that had started in the heart of the city within a few minutes after the Associated Press flash at 9:35 A.M. had given the world its first news of the surrender. For six hours Times Square was closed to all vehicular traffic by a crowd that the police placed at 500,000 between noon and 1 P.M., but by 4:30 P.M. the police had cleared the streets sufficiently for street cars and buses to operate.

"Jubilation in the other areas in which crowds gathered, such as the district centering about Wall and Broad Streets, the Borough Hall section of Brooklyn, Union, Madison and Herald Squares, and the garment manufacturing center in the West Thirties, followed an almost identical pattern. Along Fifth Avenue, on the other hand, the excitement never attained the crescendo that it did elsewhere.

"Perhaps the best index to New York's reception of the news was to be found in the strain it placed on the city's communications and transportation systems. When the flash reached them, millions of persons reached for their telephones, either to seek confirmation or to pass the glad tidings to friends or relatives. The result was to give the New York Telephone Company one of the busiest days in its history. Between 8 A.M. and noon, a record four-hour total of 1,163,470 calls was handled by the company, and it appeared last evening that the all-time high mark for a single day of 11,820,978 calls set last Sept. 14, the day of the hurricane, probably had been surpassed. At the peak the calls were coming in so rapidly that many delays in service resulted, and local broadcasting stations were asked to appeal to the public to avoid making any but essential calls.

"Soon after the long-awaited news came, the influx into such mid-Manhattan points as Rockefeller Center and Times Square placed an exceptionally heavy strain on the city's rapid transit system. By calling in workers from their days off, however, the Board of Transportation was able to put extra trains into service that coped with the rush. At 11:30 A.M. the board said that about 25,000 persons were clogging the Times Square subway stations, but nevertheless normal service was being maintained.

"Only the usual handful of morning idlers was watching *The New York Times* bulletins on Times Tower when the electrifying news was posted there. Their outward response was not spectacular, but from mouth to mouth the news spread with astonishing speed. Meanwhile, from offices and loft buildings, thousands who had heard it on the radio were pouring into the streets and the crowds grew steadily larger until the police estimated that 500,000 were in the Times Square area. A few blocks to the south, in the garment district, the enthusiasm reached an even more ecstatic level. From their loft windows towering many stories above the street, workers threw odds and ends of brightly colored materials into the breeze. Then they dropped their work and rushed pell-mell into the sunshine to help celebrate."

Broadway was lit up for the first time for years. So was the Statue of Liberty.

In Seattle, Boeing employees wheeled out a giant B-29 bomber carrying an "On To Tokyo" sign.

In Philadelphia, crowds lined the streets a dozen deep to catch a special tickertape parade. They cheered as trams rolled by carrying soldiers returned from Europe.

Anne Relph remembered being on a train with her grandmother, riding through Louisiana: "And hearing bells as we went through the little towns ... I didn't know what was going on until the train stopped and someone told us that the war in Europe had ended. There was rejoicing, sort of dancing in the street and church bells ringing in every little town we went through. In New Orleans, people were literally dancing in the streets. They were singing and dancing, jumping in and out of fountains. It was like Mardi Gras, and just this incredible sense of relief that part of our war, anyway, was finished."

Commander of the Allied Expeditionary Forces in Europe General Dwight D. Eisenhower

Men and women of the Allied Expeditionary Force:

The crusade on which we embarked in the early summer of 1944 has reached its glorious conclusion. It is my especial privilege, in the name of all nations represented in this theatre of war, to command each of you for valiant performance of duty. Though these words are feeble they come from the bottom of a heart overflowing with pride in your loyal service and admiration for you as warriors.

Your accomplishments at sea, in the air, on the ground and in the field of supply have astonished the world. Even before the final week of the conflict, you had put 5,000,000 of the enemy permanently out of the war. You have taken in stride military tasks so difficult as to be classed by many doubters as impossible. You have confused, defeated and destroyed your savagely fighting foe. On the road to victory you have endured every discomfort and privation and have surmounted every obstacle ingenuity and desperation could throw in your path. You did not pause until our front was firmly joined up with the great Red Army coming from the east, and other Allied forces, coming from the south.

Full victory in Europe has been attained.

Working and fighting together in a single and indestructible partnership you have achieved a perfection in unification of air, ground and naval power that will stand as a model in our time.

The route you have travelled through hundreds of miles is marked by the graves of former comrades. From them has been exacted the ultimate sacrifice; blood of many nations – American, British, Canadian, French, Polish and others – has helped to gain the victory. Each of the fallen died as a member of the team to which you belong, bound together by a common love of liberty and a refusal to submit to enslavement. No monument of stone, no memorial of whatever magnitude could so well express our respect and veneration for their sacrifice as would perpetuation of the spirit of comradeship in which they died. As we celebrate Victory in Europe let us remind ourselves that our common problems of the immediate and distant future can best be solved in the same conceptions of cooperation and devotion to the cause of human freedom as have made this Expeditionary Force such a mighty engine of righteous destruction.

Let us have no part in the profitless quarrels in which other men will inevitably engage as to what country, what service, won the European war. Every man, every woman, of every nation here represented, has served according to his or her ability, and the efforts of each have contributed to the outcome. This we shall remember – and in doing so we shall be revering such honoured graves and be sending comfort to the loved ones of comrades who could not live to see this day.

SALTY O'ROURKE
CHARLIE SPIVAK
JO STAFFORD
DEAN MURPHY
ALAN LADD
RUSSELL
SALTY O'ROURKE
IN PERSON
CHARLIE SPIVAK
JO STAFFORD
McBRIDE'S

"Thousands who had heard it on the radio were pouring into the streets and the crowds grew steadily larger until the police estimated that 500,000 were in the Times Square area."

The New York Times

An excerpt from President Harry Truman's news conference on VE Day

Well, I want to start off by reading you a little statement here. I want you to understand, at the very beginning, that this press conference is held with the understanding that any and all information given you here is for release at 9am this morning, eastern war time. There should be no indication of the news given here, or speculation about it, either in the press or on the radio before 9 o'clock this morning.

The radio – my radio remarks, and telegrams of congratulation to the Allied military leaders, are for release at the same time. Mr Daniels has copies of my remarks, available for you in the lobby as you go out, and also one or two releases here.

Now, for your benefit, because you won't get a chance to listen over the radio, I am going to read you the proclamation, and the principal remarks. It won't take but seven minutes, so you needn't be uneasy. You have plenty of time. [Laughter]

This is a solemn but glorious hour. General Eisenhower informs me that the forces of Germany have surrendered to the united nations. The flags of freedom fly all over Europe.

It's celebrating my birthday, too – today, too.

Voices: Happy birthday, Mr President! [Laughter]

Truman: For this victory, we join in offering our thanks to the Providence which has guided and sustained us through the dark days of adversity. Our rejoicing is sobered and subdued by a supreme consciousness of the terrible price we have paid to rid the world of Hitler and his evil band. Let us not forget, my fellow Americans, the sorrow and the heartache which today abide in the homes of so many of our neighbours – neighbours whose most priceless possession has been rendered as a sacrifice to redeem our liberty.

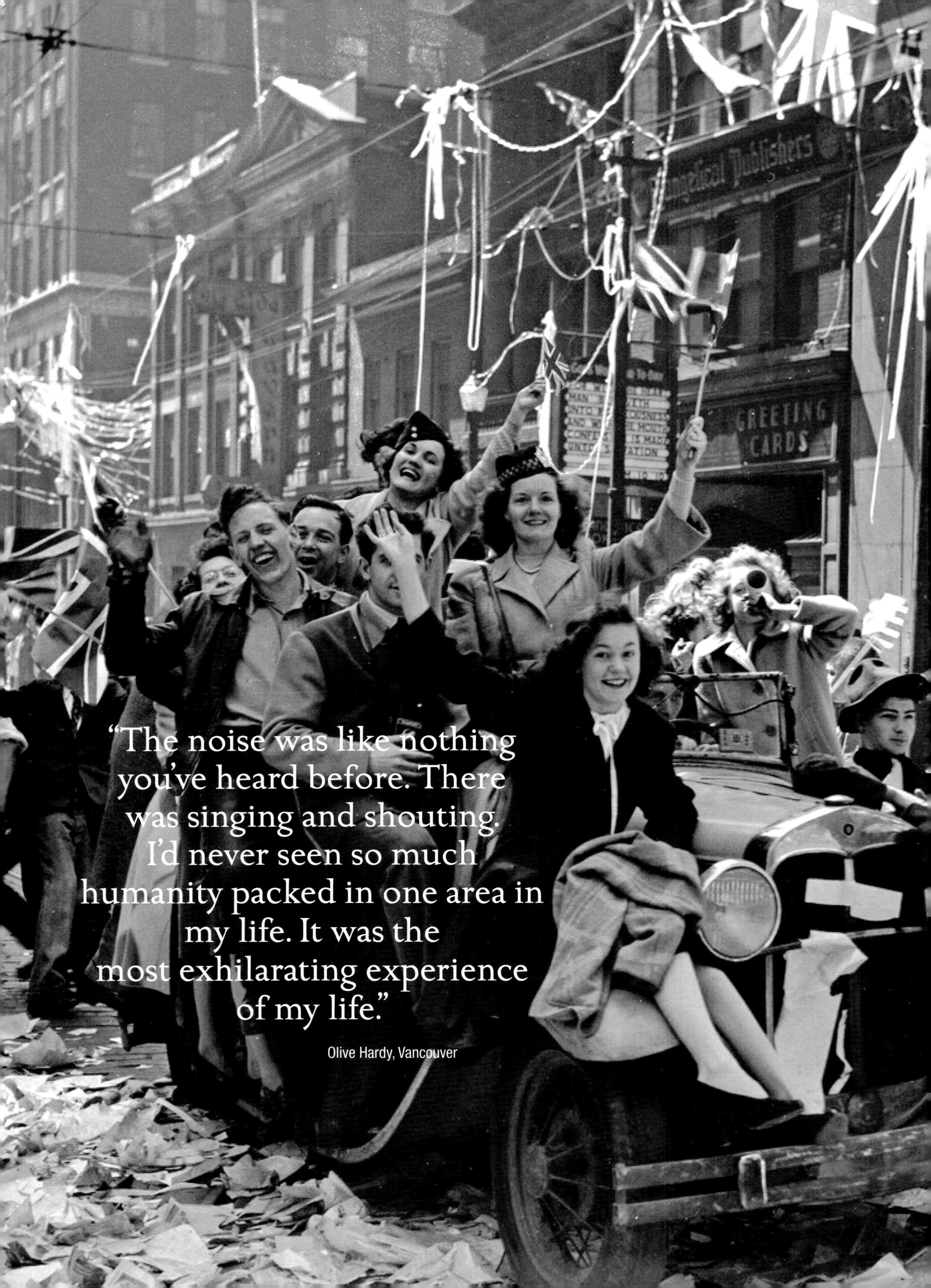

"The noise was like nothing you've heard before. There was singing and shouting. I'd never seen so much humanity packed in one area in my life. It was the most exhilarating experience of my life."

Olive Hardy, Vancouver

Canada

Canada, as a close ally of Britain, had declared war on Germany on 10 September 1939. It was the country's first independent declaration of war.

By the end of the war, more than a million Canadians had gone to fight.

The news of the Allied victory in Europe drove Canadians to the streets in celebration.

In Toronto, people danced and kissed strangers. They waved flags and streamers. On Bay Street and Yonge Street, thousands joined parades.

On 8 May, the official day of celebration, the City of Toronto organised concerts, parades, religious services and fireworks in the parks.

It was a similar scene in Vancouver. Fifty years later an 81-year- old Olive Hardie told *The Vancouver Sun* what it was like to be there: "It was just amazing going across the Burrad Bridge. There were all these people, and the excitement was sort of warming up as you went along. All these cars started wheeling on down. The toilet paper is what got me... they were throwing [rolls] up in the air, it was draped on the mid-section. You were wading through it; on the way back, it was deeper still.

"The noise was like nothing you've heard before. There was singing and shouting. I'd never seen so much humanity packed in one area in my life. It was the most exhilarating experience of my life."

But not every VE Day celebration was friendly.

In Halifax, Nova Scotia, what began as typical festivities turned into a riot as several thousand servicemen and civilians looted the city.

The city was already thick with tension even before the events of 7 and 8 May 1945. Over the course of the war, Halifax had become an overcrowded and underserviced port. Its population had doubled, but its services and infrastructure had failed to keep up.

Landlords were charging huge rents for tiny rooms. Men in uniform would be constantly cheated by shopkeepers who took one look at the uniform and raised prices.

And there was nowhere legal to get a drink (but plenty of illegal places if an enterprising soldier knew who to ask).

The news of Germany's surrender came through to soldiers in Halifax on the evening of 7 May. Rear-Admiral Leonard W. Murray overruled senior officers and allowed 9000 men under his command to head into town and enjoy the evening. However, they were warned to "be joyful without being destructive or distasteful".

By midnight, Halifax was bustling. But without any licensed bars, soldiers began to get agitated. They started a riot, setting fire to trams, looting liquor stores and stripping shops of merchandise.

When he read about what had happened in the next morning's newspapers, Murray was not convinced it was his soldiers who had misbehaved. He thought perhaps the locals were again blaming "foreign soldiers", as they tended to do when things went wrong. So he didn't rescind his order and allowed another 9500 soldiers to go ashore for the official VE Day festivities of 8 May.

By the time the mayhem had died down that evening, and soldiers were ordered off the streets with a citywide curfew in place, three men had died (two with alcohol poisoning, another a possible murder) and 363 were arrested.

Australia & N.Z.

In Australia, the war with Japan was literally closer to home, and the *Sydney Morning Herald* posed the question: "Since when has it been customary to celebrate victory halfway through a contest?" Australian troops were still fighting, and others were still prisoners of war in Japanese camps. One reader of the *Argus* complained on 11 May about the lack of VE Day celebrations in Melbourne: "Thank goodness we had the wireless to cheer us on Wednesday recording the joyousness in England. Here it was more like a solemn funeral than a great victory achieved."

Subsequent VE Days were often quiet affairs in Australian towns and cities.

In New Zealand, victory was celebrated on 9 May in an orderly fashion – the government having made detailed plans months in advance – and the population quietly obeyed instructions.

Berlin

After the success of the Victory Parade, the Soviets proposed another parade for 7 September in Berlin, which would feature soldiers from all Allied powers – the Soviet Union, the United States, Britain and France.

Much of the German capital lay in ruins, with recovery efforts well under way. The parade was held near the Reichstag building and the Brandenburg Gate.

Zhukov was again one of the most senior officers who attended. Beside him was General George Patton of the US, General Brian Robertson of Britain and General Marie-Pierre Koenig from France. Patton and Robertson were actually replacements, as Generals Eisenhower and Montgomery declined invitations to attend.

About 5000 troops took part, 2000 of them representing the Soviet Union. Units included the Soviet 248th Infantry Division, the French 2nd Infantry Division, the British 131st Infantry Brigade and the US 82nd Airborne Division. Other soldiers marching that day came from garrisons in the occupied city.

The parade was much more heavily publicised on the Soviet side. In what may be seen as an early indicator of the Cold War to come, the 1945 Berlin Victory Parade was played down by the West. Tensions were already developing over what was to be done with Berlin and Soviet-occupied parts of eastern Europe. For the West, far greater attention was given to parades the following year – in Berlin on the first anniversary of VE Day, and the London Victory Celebrations of 8 June 1946.

Elsewhere in Germany, members of the American 101st Airborne Division enjoyed drinks where Hitler had held high-level meetings – the "Eagle's Nest", his mountaintop retreat in Berchtesgaden in the Bavarian Alps. The town was also the southern headquarters of the Nazi Party.

After taking part in the Normandy invasion, units of the 101st Airborne trekked through Europe, fighting enemy forces wherever they found them, particularly in Bastogne, Belgium, where Hitler's last western offensive was turned back during the Battle of the Bulge in December 1944.

Months later, with the war winding down, the Allies recognised the need to take Berchtesgaden to prevent it being used by diehard Nazis for guerrilla operations run by the SS. By that time, however, Hitler had been discovered dead in Berlin and German troops were surrendering en masse. Berchtesgaden was no longer a strategic objective. Instead, it became the ultimate trophy for Allied forces.

The 101st Airborne's Company E was among the first American units to reach the Eagle's Nest in a race against Russian and French troops. If Berchtesgaden still held any spiritual significance for true believers across Germany, a lingering Allied presence there would go a long way toward crushing it.

The troops went through the abandoned homes of Nazi officials and confiscated thousands of bottles of Europe's best wines. Accounts put Goering's stock at 10,000 to 16,000 bottles. After VE Day Allied units were rewarded with their own tour of Berchtesgaden and by the time Eisenhower arrived the town had been stripped of all moveable objects.

Any item with a swastika was allowed to be taken. Troops took trays of silverware adorned with an eagle and swastika bracketed with the initials "A H." Gold-trimmed white Nazi ceremonial flags, candelabra, linen, china and crystal were among the items found. There was so much booty that the occupying troops played cards using it as currency.

Moscow

Victory Day marks the capitulation of Nazi Germany to the Soviet Union.

It is celebrated on 9 May, a day after the western Allies mark VE Day, because the Kremlin was unhappy that General Ivan Susloparov had been the only Soviet representative at the first German surrender in Reims.

Stalin ordered another surrender next day, in a surviving manor on the outskirts of Berlin. There, German Field Marshal Wilhelm Keitel again submitted his country's capitulation, this time to Soviet Marshal Georgy Zhukov, a more appropriately ranked member of Soviet command in the eyes of the Kremlin.

The Soviet population got the news of end of the "The Great Patriotic War" in much the same way as the British: by radio broadcast.

At 8pm on 9 May, Stalin addressed the nation. "Comrades! Men and women compatriots. The great day of victory over Germany has come."

Jubilant Russians spilled on to the streets of Moscow. Red Square became full of men and women laughing, cheering, singing patriotic songs and dancing.

The first Victory Parade was held several weeks later, on 24 June. It allowed enough time for soldiers to return to Moscow from where they had been fighting.

Stalin ordered the parade on 22 June: "Order of the Supreme Commander in Chief, Armed Forces of the USSR and concurrent People's Commissar of State for National Defence.

"To mark the victory over Germany in the Great Patriotic War, I order a parade of troops of the Army, Navy and the Moscow Garrison, the Victory Parade, on June 24, 1945, at Moscow's Red Square.

"Marching on parade shall be the combined regiments of all the fronts, a People's Commissariat of National Defence combined regiment, the Soviet Navy, military academies and schools, and troops of the Moscow Garrison and Military District."

Zhukov, the man who had accepted the second of the two German surrenders, rode at the parade. Joining him on white and black stallions was Konstantin Rokossovsky, a prominent Red Army officer who had been a key in the conquest of German-occupied Poland and Belarus.

Stalin stood atop Lenin's mausoleum and watched the parade beside other high-ranking Soviet Union and Red Army officials. There is some suggestion that he may have originally planned to involve himself more directly in the parade. Zhukov's memoirs suggest Stalin wanted to lead, but fell from his horse during the rehearsal, which is why the honour went to Zhukov. Critics, such as former spy Viktor Suvorov, disagree, saying the story was invented.

After the troops' parade, soldiers put banners of Nazi Germany next to Lenin's tomb. One belonged to the 1st SS Division Leibstandarte SS Adolf Hitler, the personal bodyguards of the now dead German leader.

Despite the pomp and ceremony of the parade, it would have been far more spectacular in better weather. Persistent rain and grey skies meant the flypast and civil parade had to be cancelled.

Joseph Stalin's Victory Day broadcast

COMRADES! Men and women compatriots!

The great day of victory over Germany has come. Fascist Germany, forced to her knees by the Red Army and the troops of our Allies, has acknowledged herself defeated and declared unconditional surrender.

On May 7 the preliminary protocol on surrender was signed in the city of Reims. On May 8 representatives of the German High Command, in the presence of representatives of the Supreme Command of the Allied troops and the Supreme Command of the Soviet Troops, signed in Berlin the final act of surrender, the execution of which began at 24.00 hours on May 8.

Being aware of the wolfish habits of the German ringleaders, who regard treaties and agreements as empty scraps of paper, we have no reason to trust their words. However, this morning, in pursuance of the act of surrender, the German troops began to lay down their arms and surrender to our troops en masse. This is no longer an empty scrap of paper. This is actual surrender of Germany's armed forces. True, one group of German troops in the area of Czechoslovakia is still evading surrender. But I trust that the Red Army will be able to bring it to its senses.

Now we can state with full justification that the historic day of the final defeat of Germany, the day of the great victory of our people over German imperialism has come.

The great sacrifices we made in the name of the freedom and independence of our Motherland, the incalculable privations and sufferings experienced by our people in the course of the war, the intense work in the rear and at the front, placed on the altar of the Motherland, have not been in vain, and have been crowned by complete victory over the enemy. The age-long struggle of the Slav peoples for their existence and their independence has ended in victory over the German invaders and German tyranny.

Henceforth the great banner of the freedom of the peoples and peace among peoples will fly over Europe.

Three years ago Hitler declared for all to hear that his aims included the dismemberment of the Soviet Union and the wresting from it of the Caucasus, the Ukraine, Byelorussia, the Baltic lands and other areas. He declared bluntly: "We will destroy Russia so that she will never be able to rise again." This was three years ago. However, Hitler's crazy ideas were not fated to come true—the progress of the war scattered them to the winds. In actual fact the direct opposite of the Hitlerites' ravings has taken place. Germany is utterly defeated. The German troops are surrendering. The Soviet Union is celebrating Victory, although it does not intend either to dismember or to destroy Germany.

Comrades! The Great Patriotic War has ended in our complete victory. The period of war in Europe is over. The period of peaceful development has begun.

I congratulate you upon victory, my dear men and women compatriots!

Glory to our heroic Red Army, which upheld the independence of our Motherland and won victory over the enemy! Glory to our great people, the people victorious! Eternal glory to the heroes who fell in the struggle against the enemy and gave their lives for the freedom and happiness of our people!

Aftermath

Great Britain

Churchill's Conservative Party was expected to win the post-war election easily. His strong leadership and resolve had been a huge influence in the victory. But in a sign that Britain wanted to move on and begin rebuilding, the Labour Party won 393 seats, an increase of 239. Churchill's Conservatives lost 190 seats.

However, the optimism of the new Government being able to follow through on its promised social reforms was short-lived. In September 1945, the American Lend Lease program ended, dealing a severe blow to the economy. The Government was eventually able to secure a loan from the Americans in July 1946, which shored up the economy. Even so, rationing continued for several years after the war.

The Soviet Union

The Soviets had paid a huge price for putting so many bodies in front of the German guns. Almost 9 million soldiers died in combat. But 19 million civilian lives were lost in the Great Patriotic War. Even by wartime standards, the Soviet people had done it tough. Millions had died from bombings, mass shootings, genocide and starvation in besieged cities such as Stalingrad.

The loss of life was so bad that the Soviet Union's population did not return to pre-war levels for 30 years.

Many Soviet soldiers were suspected of having collaborated with the Nazis during captivity. About 225,000 were sent to forced labour camps, with many others conscripted back into the Red Army.

The economy was in tatters. About a quarter of total capital resources were gone, and industrial and agricultural output were well below pre-war levels.

But the USSR had gained a lot of land. As well as reclaiming territory lost to the Germans in the early months of the war, the Red Army had swept through Poland, Hungary, Czechoslovakia, Romania, Yugoslavia, Albania, Bulgaria and the eastern part of Germany.

The alliance between the western Allies and the Soviet Union collapsed over what to do with these territories. The breaking point was Poland: the Soviets blocked the Polish Government in Exile from returning to power, and set up a Provisional Council sympathetic to Russia.

Communism was about to be forcefully introduced in eastern Europe. The Soviets aided local communist organisations to take power in these countries. They came to be known as "satellite states" and helped secure a greater buffer between the Western capitalist nations and Moscow.

Sensing the danger to global peace and democracy, Winston Churchill warned the West of what the future would bring when he spoke at Westminster College in Missouri in March 1946: "From

Stettin in the Baltic to Trieste in the Adriatic, an iron curtain has descended across the Continent. Behind that line lie all the capitals of the ancient states of Central and Eastern Europe. Warsaw, Berlin, Prague, Vienna, Budapest, Belgrade, Bucharest and Sofia, all these famous cities and the populations around them lie in what I must call the Soviet sphere, and all are subject in one form or another, not only to Soviet influence but to a very high and, in many cases, increasing measure of control from Moscow."

The Soviet grab for control over eastern Europe set the stage for the Cold War.

United States

More than 200,000 American soldiers died in the European theatre of World War II. But the end of the war in Europe did not mean war was over for the US.

The tide in the Pacific had slowly been turning in the Americans' favour. The Imperial Japanese Army was in retreat across South-East Asia and the Pacific. What's more, in February 1945, President Roosevelt had reached an agreement with the Soviet Union for the Red Army to enter the Pacific conflict. They did so on 9 August 1945, 90 days after the war ended in Europe, by invading Manchuria. It was the day the second atomic bomb was dropped, on Nagasaki.

On 12 April, Roosevelt died at age 63. Vice President Harry Truman became President. Just as America's war was reaching its climax, he had to make his most difficult decision as Commander-in-Chief.

Now on the offensive, the Americans faced two broad choices. If the Japanese were refusing total surrender, then the fight would need to be taken to the main islands. The Allied forces could launch a full-scale invasion of Japan, which would mean a huge loss of life to both Japan and the US, both military and civilian.

The other option was to reveal to the world what scientists had been working on since 1942. Afraid that the Germans would get there first, the US government had poured billions of dollars into the research and development of a nuclear bomb.

On 6 August 1945 a single plane dropped an atomic bomb on the Japanese port city of Hiroshima. It was the first nuclear bomb attack in history. Three days later, another bomb was dropped on Nagasaki. The bombs obliterated the two cities. Between 140,000 and 240,000 people are estimated to have died, either from the immediate blasts or the exposure to radiation.

Japan surrendered on 15 August 1945.

Europe

The Allies established administrations in Austria and Germany. Austria became a neutral state, non-aligned with any political bloc. Germany was divided into western and eastern zones controlled by the Allies and the USSR respectively. A denazification program in Germany led to the prosecution of Nazi war criminals and the removal of ex-Nazis from power, although this policy moved towards amnesty and re-integration of ex-Nazis into West German society.

Germany lost a quarter of its 1937 territory. Among the eastern territories, Silesia, Neumark and most of Pomerania were taken over by Poland, East Prussia was divided between Poland and the USSR, followed by the expulsion of the nine million Germans from these provinces, as well as the expulsion to Germany of three million Germans from the Sudetenland in Czechoslovakia. By the 1950s, every fifth West German was a refugee from the east. The Soviet Union also took over the Polish provinces east of the Curzon line, from which two million Poles were expelled. North-east Romania, parts of

201

THE GARDEN
OF INSIDE-OUTSIDE

In early 1979, after reigning for thirty-seven years, the Shah of Iran was overthrown by the Islamic Revolution and fled the country. Days later, one of his chief enemies, Ayatollah Khomeini, returned after fourteen years in exile, the last few months of which were spent in France. He became known as the "Guide of the Revolution" and founded the Islamic Republic of Iran. Religious authority controlled all institutions. The country descended into chaos.

On 4 November 1979, following an attack on the American embassy in the capital, Tehran, fifty-two American diplomats and citizens were taken hostage by student supporters of Khomeini, who were demanding that the Shah return to face trial. The Americans were held as prisoners for 444 days, during what became known as the "hostage crisis".

In September 1980, Iraq, led by Saddam Hussein, took advantage of Iran's political instability by invading. This marked the start of a bloody war that would last eight years.

It was during these disturbing historical events that my father, Francesco Mezzalama, was appointed Italy's ambassador to Iran. He took up his post in Tehran at the end of November 1980, in the thick of the revolution, the hostage crisis and the war. My mother, my brother and I joined him at the embassy a few months later, for the summer of 1981. Which is where this story begins...

Chiara Mezzalama

LEAVING

One day, my father told us we were going to a faraway country. I packed my suitcase on a summer's evening. My little brother and I chose a few toys and some cards and books. We weren't sure if we'd find any, where we were going.

There was an inside and an outside, where we were going...

INSIDE

There was once a garden. A garden so huge it was never-ending. A wild garden, where princes and princesses used to live. Real ones, not the sort you find in made-up stories.

That garden held memories, fountains the colour of the sky, pomegranate trees, tall grasses where all kinds of insects hid, wild flowers and a pond with a carp that was one hundred years old.

Tall plane trees, with leaves as big as giants' hands, offered shelter for the birds flying through the clouds. They would land in the branches and hold their conferences. It was a garden full of hiding places.

OUTSIDE

Before our arrival, the garden was neglected. The princes and princesses had been driven out and the huge iron gates locked. The city where this secret garden belonged had collapsed into war, and nobody heard the birds singing any more or the water in the fountains. Even the wind in the leaves of those massive trees was silent. Gunfire, exploding bombs and cries drowned out every sound.

The city had grown dark. So had its women and men. People queued for food. Everywhere there were soldiers with heavy boots and big beards, their rifles slung across their shoulders. The city-monster made us feel very frightened.

INSIDE

But we were safe inside our garden. A wall protected us from the city-monster. We set off on adventures to the other end of the grounds: we were so far away from the house, we felt as if we were all alone in the world, with our rubber boots and our sticks. We chased butterflies, caught lizards and picked wild flowers for our mother.

We didn't have any friends, so we asked for a dog.
And we got one! A small yellow dog who ran about with us like a mad thing. There were three of us now, and we were happy.

In the evenings, the scent of jasmine flowers would fill the garden. We ate outside, by candlelight, to the sounds of the fountains and a concert of cicadas.

OUTSIDE

Sometimes we heard air-raid sirens. Bombs would explode in the city-monster, and the rattle of gunfire would wake us in the middle of the night. Our mother came to reassure us. She held us very tightly in her arms.

"Why do people wage wars?" I used to ask her.
"Sometimes, people grow mad – with anger, with hatred – they lose their grip on words and choose weapons instead. The truth is I don't know the answer to your question," she replied.

Our mother became sad. She reacted by scolding the crows which ate her flowers and left pink and purple bird-droppings all over the garden. She would clap her hands, but the crows knew they were safe inside our walls.

INSIDE

One day, the dog, my little brother and I set off for an adventure at the bottom of the garden. The wild grasses were tall and dry; they scratched our legs.

At the bottom of the garden stood the iron gates, which were always locked. We peered through them and glimpsed the other side. We could hear the city-monster breathing darkly.

A little boy peered back. He was staring at us from the other side of the bars.
Then, quick as a cat, he climbed the wall and leapt into our garden.
He held out his hand towards us. My brother and the dog ran off, but I stayed there. His hand felt warm in mine.
We didn't speak the same language, but I understood that we'd become friends.
He put his hand to his chest and told me his name: "Massoud."
AND I'M CHIARA.

OUTSIDE - INSIDE

"Are you mad?" my little brother wanted to know. "His father might be a revolutionary, one of the bloodthirsty beards. If it was so easy for him to climb the wall, what's to stop others? We simply have to tell the grown-ups!"

That night, I felt a little frightened: my brother was right, our protecting wall had been breached. There was no longer an inside and an outside. The city-monster was spreading its tentacles.

The next day, I set off in search of my new friend at the bottom of the garden. There he was, waiting for me, with his beaten-up shoes, his torn T-shirt, his tousled hair, his dark eyes. He looked handsome.

Together, we mounted our horses and travelled along the silk roads. He was the Persian prince of Outside-Inside, with his sabre and talking bird.

I was the lion-taming princess and snake-charming enchantress. All the treasures from the Kingdom of Inside-Outside belonged to me.

Our evil enemies wore beards and turbans. They loathed music, so we sang. They loathed dancing, so we danced. They were afraid of beauty, so we picked flowers to adorn our hair.

We climbed a fig tree to gather its fruit, which tasted of sugar and sunshine. We ran, we jumped, we watched the clouds moving across the sky. Massoud could come into the garden, but I couldn't venture out.

INSIDE - OUTSIDE
I wanted to find a present for Massoud, to give him something special because he was my friend.
I took off my favourite T-shirt, the one with lots of different colours.
And I gave it to him.
He stared at me with a serious expression and shook his head.
Then he fled.

The T-shirt was left behind, in the dust.
DON'T YOU WANT IT?
WHY NOT?
I was angry, I shouted, I wept.
Inside-outside, inside-outside... Those words were going round and round inside my head, until they gave me a headache.

That was when I understood how hard it was to mix inside and outside. The wall had a good side and a bad side. But who says which side of the wall you're on? Who gets to choose?

I didn't want to run down to the bottom of the garden any more.
I spent my days reading, while my little brother played with the dog.

I felt sad and locked away, as if in a golden prison.

Then one day I made up my mind and I set off again.
There was Massoud, in my colourful T-shirt - he looked great in it. He was holding something in his hand.
It was for me.
A tiny cat carved out of wood.

I stared at it, felt it,
and hid it at the bottom
of my pocket.
It wasn't a gift,
it was a swap.
OUR
INSIDE-OUTSIDE
SECRET.
He nodded, smiled at me and left.

RETURNING

We left that faraway country. The war there ended a long time ago. The garden is even more beautiful now, filled with flowers, trees, fountains and birds (yes, and crows too).

Sometimes I think of Massoud, and I wonder what happened to him. Did he keep the secret of inside-outside?

When I'm feeling unsure about anything, I hold his little cat tightly at the bottom of my pocket. I think of Massoud and then I'm brave enough to breach walls. Because there are so many walls, everywhere you go.

There are insides where we feel safe and outsides that make us feel frightened. There are walls and there are cats, as brave as you, and him, and me, leaping from one side to the other.

This edition first published in 2020 by Book Island

info@bookisland.co.uk

This edition was published by arrangement with The Picture Book Agency, France.

First published in French as *Le jardin du dedans-dehors*

Edited by Victoria Millar

Typeset by Matthew Kelly

British Library Cataloguing-in-Publication Data

A CIP record for this title is available from the British Library.

Co-funded by the
Creative Europe Programme
of the European Union

Printed in Latvia on FSC certified paper

ISBN: 978-1-911496-16-8

Book Island is a small, independent publishing house, based in Bristol.

Visit www.bookisland.co.uk for more information about our books.